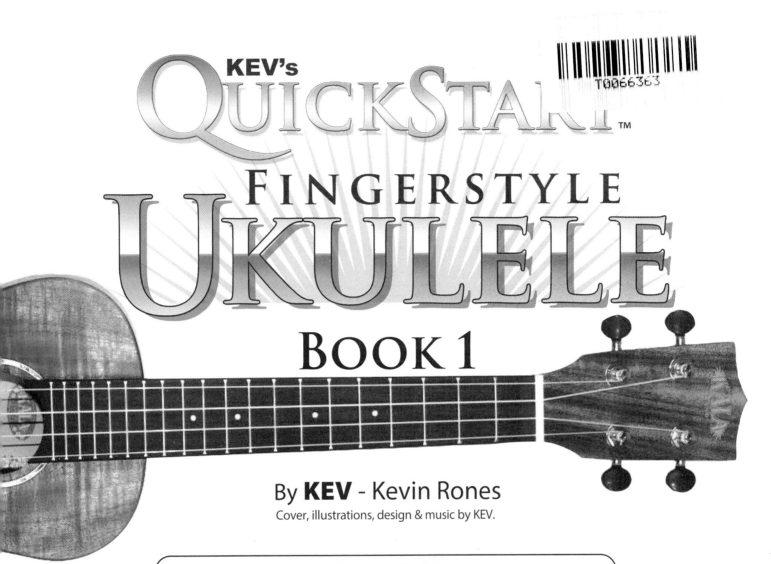

KEV's QuickStart™
FINGERSTYLE UKULELE
BOOK 1

By **KEV** - Kevin Rones

Cover, illustrations, design & music by KEV.

To access audio visit:

www.halleonard.com/mylibrary

Enter Code
6673-6055-5063-6842

ISBN 978-1-57424-278-2
SAN 683-8022

CENTERSTREAM®

Table of Contents

What is Fingerstyle Ukulele?

With the help of the internet the Ukulele has begun to re-emerge as a popular instrument for songwriters, solo instrumentalists and Indie artists.

Fingerstyle Ukulele is a general term that describes the plucking of the strings with the fingers of your strumming hand using a variety of techniques.

Fingerstyle incorporates melody, chords, strumming, percussive techniques, tapping, slides, bends and pull-offs.

Fingerstyle Ukulele players can play solo pieces or accompany other players and singers. They can play *Classical*, *Jazz*, *Celtic*, *Blues*, *Rock & Roll*, *Folk*, *Indie music* and more.

Hawaiian Ukulele generally involves a variety of strumming patterns played as an accompaniment to singers and dancers who perform a series of movements that tell a story.

Slack Key is generally associated with a style of Hawaiian Guitar playing in which the strings of the guitar are tuned down, or "slackened" into different tunings. There are many styles of Slack Key, but they all share common turnarounds and patterns. Some Slack Key tunes and techniques can be adapted to be played on ukulele.

Chord Melody was adopted by jazz players as a way to play solo ukulele without a vocalist. By playing different chord inversions up and down the fretboard they were able to comp or simulate the melody line of popular jazz standards.

Melody Picking is done using a plectrum (pick) or fingers to play single melody notes. This is usually accompanied by other instrumentation.

"The Wizard of the Strings" Roy Smeck

Roy Smeck (1900-1994) was one of the original innovators on the ukulele. He started his career on the vaudeville circuit. Knowing he could not sing well, he developed his skills on guitar, banjo and ukulele and added trick playing and novelty dances to his act.

Roy was dubbed as "The Wizard of the Strings" and was one of the first to incorporate fingerstyle, tapping and percussive techniques on the ukulele.

He made over 500 recordings and wrote instructional method books and arrangements for the instruments he played. Smeck invented and endorsed the Vita-Uke and other stringed instruments. In 1926 Warner Brothers released the film *Don Juan* starring John Barrymore. It was the first feature film using the new Vitaphone sound-on-disc system. The preview to that film was a short film featuring Roy Smeck titled *His Pastimes* which made him an instant celebrity.

Tuning Your Ukulele

C tuning (High G) - G C E A

Imagine being trapped in a savage land with no smart phone reception. How can you tune your ukulele without your tuning app? You must rely on your tuning survival instincts! Like our ancestors before us... we must resort to *Relative Tuning*. With Relative tuning you can tune the ukulele to itself.

Remember with this method you may not be in tune with other instruments.
Use an electronic tuner or a tuning app to tune to ***Concert Pitch*** (A 440 Hz for **A** above Middle **C**)

Relative Tuning: Tuning without an electronic tuner or app.

About Ukulele Tunings

The exercises in this book were created for ukuleles tuned to standard C tuning using a High G (4th) string (C G E A).

This C tuning is the most common ukulele tuning and is the tuning most associated with the "ukulele sound". This C tuning is commonly referred to as C with a **"High G"** tuning because the G (4th) string has a higher pitch than the C (3rd) string.

Ukuleles are sometimes strung in C tuning with a lower pitch G (4th) string. This is known as C with a **"Low G"**. This tuning is similar to a standard guitar tuning. If your ukulele is strung with a Low G you can still practice the fingerstyle patterns in this book, the compositions however were written to take advantage of the High G tuning.

DID YOU KNOW:

When you place a capo on the fifth fret of a 6-string guitar the first four guitar strings are the same pitch as Low G tuning on a ukulele. Playing a basic **D** chord on the guitar is equivilant to a **G** chord on the ukulele.

The *Baritone Ukulele* is tuned exactly like the last 4 strings of the guitar. **D G B E**.

Step 1. Tighten the **C** (3rd) string until you feel it sounds in pitch.

Step 2. Tune the **E** (2nd) string to the pitch of the (3rd string).

Press your left index finger onto the fourth fret of the **C** string of your ukulele. This is an **E** note. Play the **E** note on string three and then strike the open **E** string. Turn the **E** string until the notes of both strings two and three sound the same.

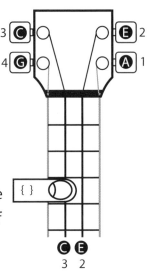

Step 3. Tune the **A** (1st) string to the pitch of the **E** (2nd) string.

Press your left index finger onto the fifth fret of the **E** (2nd) string of your ukulele. This is an **A** note. Play the **A** note on string 2 and then strike the open **A** (1st) string. Turn the **A** (1st) string until both strings two and one sound the same pitch.

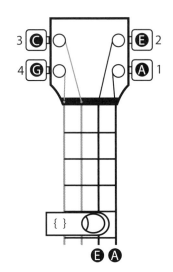

Step 4. Tune the High **G** (4th) string to the pitch of the **G** note on the (2nd) string.

Place your left index finger on the third fret of the **E** (2nd) string of your ukulele. This is a **G** note. Play the **G** note on the (2nd) string and then strike the open **G** (4th) string. Both strings should sound the same. Turn the **G** (4th) string until both strings sound the same.

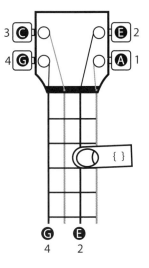

Reading a Chord Diagram

A chord diagram is a graphical representation of the ukulele fretboard from the same perspective that you would view your ukulele if it were on a stand in front of you.

> The **dots** represent where you press on the fret board to form a chord. The fretting hand fingers are numbered index 1, Middle 2, Ring 3, Pinky 4, and fretting hand Thumb T.

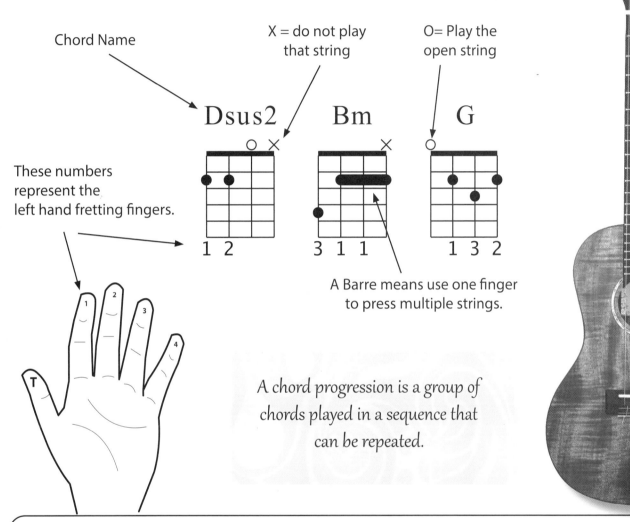

Chord Name

X = do not play that string

O= Play the open string

These numbers represent the left hand fretting fingers.

Dsus2   **Bm**   **G**

1 2   3 1 1   1 3 2

A Barre means use one finger to press multiple strings.

A chord progression is a group of chords played in a sequence that can be repeated.

Strumming the Ukulele

There are several ways to strum the ukulele. For the purposes of this book we will use the two most common strum techniques. The index brush strum is the most used technique for fingerstyle ukulele.

The Index Brush
Strum downward using the back of your fingernail at an approximate 90 degree angle to the strings.
For upstrokes use the pad of the index finger as it curls into the natural loose fist hand position.

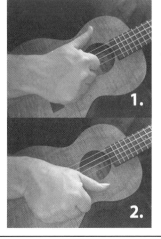

The Thumb Strum
This is the most common strum. Simply strum in a downward and upward motion with your thumb.

Knowing Your Ukulele

The Four Basic Ukulele Sizes

SOPRANO
Size: 20" *
Fretboard Length (scale):13.5"
Frets: 12-15*

Tuning
G C E A

CONCERT
Size: 24" *
Fretboard Length (scale):15"
Frets: 15-17*

Tuning
G C E A

TENOR
Size: 26" *
Fretboard Length (scale):17"
Frets: 18-20*

Tuning
G C E A

BARITONE
Size: 30" *
Fretboard Length (scale):19"
Frets: 19-20*

Tuning
D G B E

* Length and fret numbers can vary between ukulele builders.

Soprano
The Soprano or Standard size ukulele is the smallest and most widely owned ukulele. They are very portable and are usually the least expensive. They produce a higher "treble" sound commonly associated with ukulele. Soprano sized ukuleles are most commonly tuned in standard C6 (High G) tuning.

Concert
The Concert ukulele is sometimes referred to as the Alto Ukulele. It is a little larger than a Soprano Ukulele with a slightly fuller sound. Concert Ukuleles have a higher string tension and wider frets. There can be up to 20 frets on a Concert Ukulele. Concert sized ukuleles are usually tuned in standard C6 (High G) tuning, however some people prefer C6 (Low G) tuning in which the G string is tuned down an octave.

Tenor
Tenor ukuleles are larger than Concert sized ukuleles. Because of its rich full sound, and additional frets the Tenor is the popular choice for fingerstyle ukulele enthusiasts. Tenor sized ukuleles are usually tuned in standard C6 (High G) tuning, however some people prefer C6 (Low G) tuning in which the G string is tuned down an octave.

Baritone
The Baritone ukulele is a little bigger than the Tenor sized ukuleles. It is tuned exactly like the top four strings on a guitar. D G B E. It is sometimes referred to as "the little guitar".

The Baritone Ukulele - A Cautionary Tale.

The **Baritone Ukulele** is tuned to **D G B E**. This is the same tuning as the 4 higher strings of the guitar. The **D G B E** tuning is also used for Tenor guitars.

A common mistake that beginning ukulele players make when purchasing their first ukulele is choosing a Baritone, because they like its "deeper" sound without understanding that *the Baritone Ukulele* is tuned like a *Tenor guitar*, and not like a *Tenor Ukulele G C E A*.

While a Baritone ukulele sounds great - it is not a standard tuned ukulele. You should be aware that the chord names for *Baritone Ukulele are different than the chords played on Standard Tuned (GCEA) Soprano, Concert and Tenor Ukuleles*. Most ukulele books and ukulele club tune books use *Standard Ukulele* chord diagrams and **not** Baritone chords. *Start on a Standard Tuned Ukulele!*

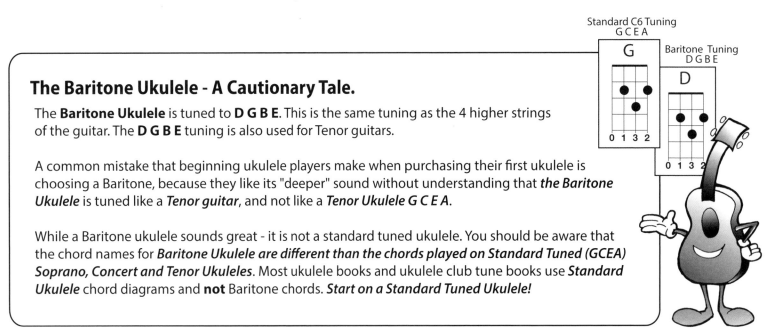

Standard C6 Tuning
G C E A

Baritone Tuning
D G B E

Strings and Things

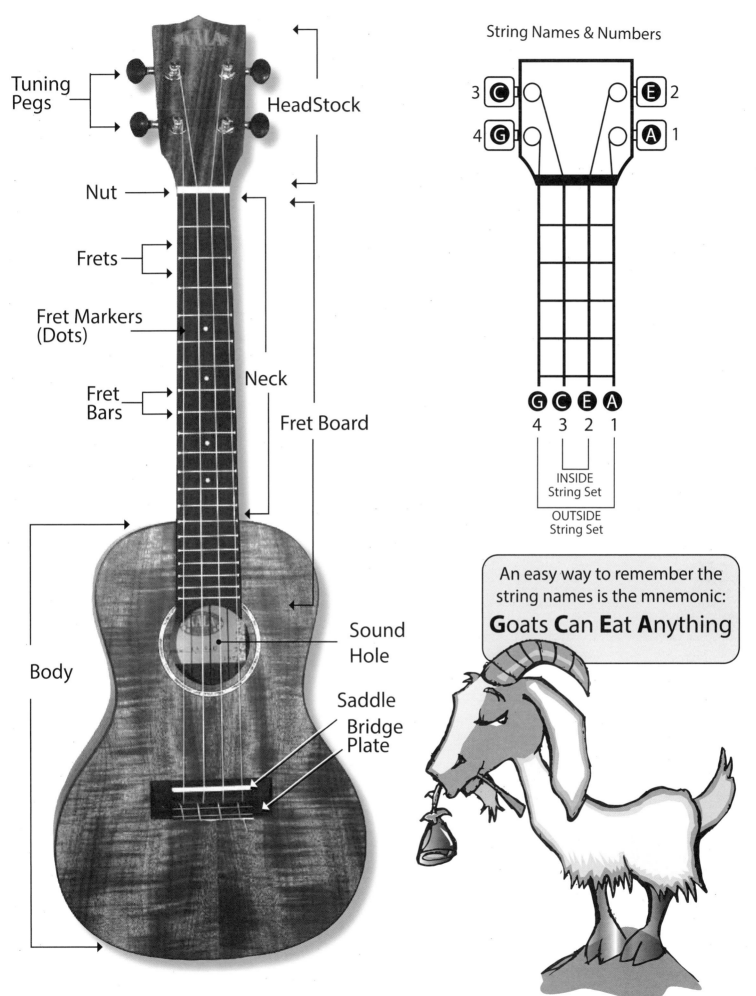

Tuning Pegs

HeadStock

Nut

Frets

Fret Markers (Dots)

Neck

Fret Bars

Fret Board

Body

Sound Hole

Saddle

Bridge Plate

String Names & Numbers

3 C   E 2
4 G   A 1

G C E A
4 3 2 1

INSIDE String Set

OUTSIDE String Set

An easy way to remember the string names is the mnemonic:

Goats **C**an **E**at **A**nything

How to Hold the Ukulele

Fingerstyle

Fingerstyle Picking Position

For fingerstyle ukulele we change the angle of the neck to a slightly higher angle between the 1 o'clock and 2 o'clock position. Note that the right forearm rests higher on the ukulele. Some people prefer to use a seated position resting the ukulele on the right thigh.

This is the position we use for this book!

Some people prefer to use a *ukulele strap* while playing fingerstyle ukulele. Make sure that it is adjusted properly so your hand is in the same proper position both seated and standing.

Traditional

Traditional Strumming Position

Normally the ukulele is cradled with the right forearm and strummed with the right hand thumb and fingers. The angle of the neck is generally between the 2 o'clock and 3 o'clock position. The right forearm holds the ukulele against the body. *Don't use this position for fingerstyle ukulele!*

Getting into Position

A key concept in fingerstyle ukulele is to use one proper hand position that can be used to easily grab each of the 4 strings for any picking patterns.

1. Place your right thumb on the **G** (4th) string and drop your fingers so they naturally fall at 90 degree angle to the strings.

2. Curl your right fingers into a loose fist.
- Make sure your right thumb *(p)* is on the **G** (4th) string.
- Place your right index *(i)* finger on string **C** (3rd) string.
- Place your right middle finger *(m)* on the **E** (2nd) string.
- Place your right ring (a) finger on the **A** (1st) string.

3. Use the pencil test to determine if your fingers are correct.
Take a pencil and point it straight down from the center of your right thumb knuckle at an approximate 90 degree angle to the ukulele strings. Your fingers can touch the pencil. *If the angle of the pencil changes, your hand position is incorrect.*

Check Your position
You should be able to press down on the G (4th) string with your thumb and apply upward pressure on the first, second and third strings.

Learning to use proper hand position may seem awkward at first but the reward is worth it!

Stick with it. Become Great.

Left and Right Hand Fingering Notation

To differentiate between the left and the right hand fingers a system of notation commonly known as **p i m a** was developed.

Learning *p i m a* notation

Using the *p i m a* system we can define through notation which right hand fingers are used to strike each of the strings.

The right hand (picking) fingers are named *p* for thumb, *i* for index, *m* for middle, *a* for the ring finger.

The left hand (fretting) fingers are named **T** for thumb, **1** for index, **2** for middle, **3** for the ring finger and **4** for the pinkie.

Left hand numbers are used in chord diagrams.

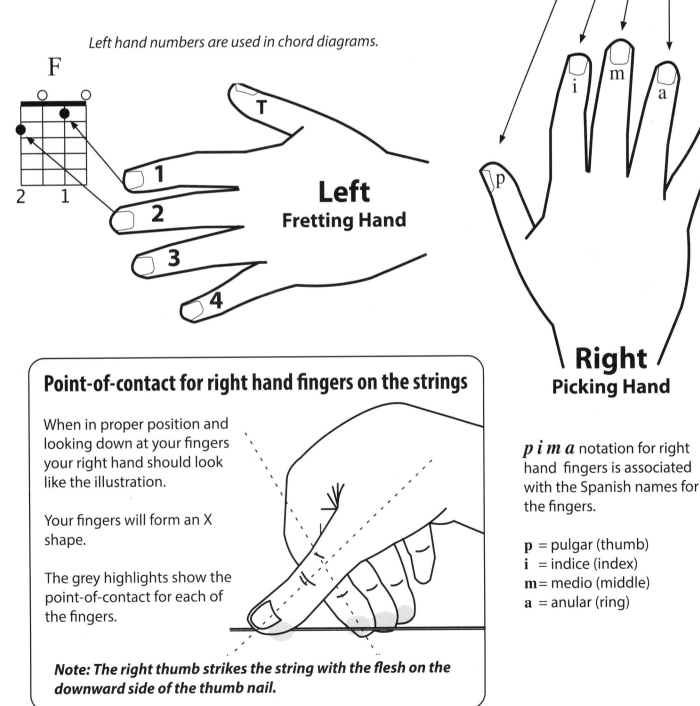

Left
Fretting Hand

Right
Picking Hand

String Names   **G C E A**
String Numbers   4   3   2   1

p i m a notation for right hand fingers is associated with the Spanish names for the fingers.

p = pulgar (thumb)
i = indice (index)
m = medio (middle)
a = anular (ring)

Point-of-contact for right hand fingers on the strings

When in proper position and looking down at your fingers your right hand should look like the illustration.

Your fingers will form an X shape.

The grey highlights show the point-of-contact for each of the fingers.

Note: The right thumb strikes the string with the flesh on the downward side of the thumb nail.

How to Read Tablature

It's easy!

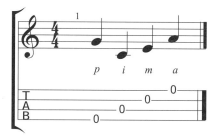

The exercises in this book are written in both *Standard Music Notation* and *Ukulele Tablature*.

The diagram on the left shows the open strings of the Ukulele in *Standard Music notation* (top) and *Tablature* or *TAB* on the bottom. The lower case letters *p i m a* refer to the right hand fingers.

Tablature or *TAB* is system of music notation that tells you which string and fret to play. Each of the four staff lines represent a string on the ukulele. The numbers on each line (string) indicate which fret to press as the string is played.

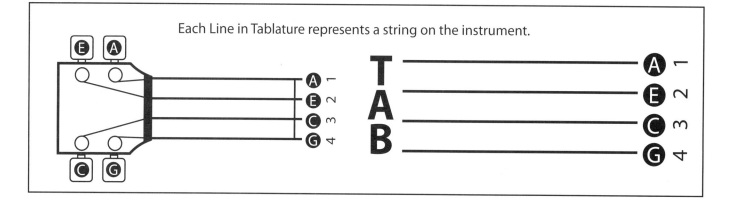

Each Line in Tablature represents a string on the instrument.

Reading your first notes in TAB

Each line represents a string on the ukulele. The numbers on the lines indicate which fret to press down on that string. In the example to the right we see the number 3 indicated on string 1 (**A**). Place your finger on the third fret of the string and play that note.

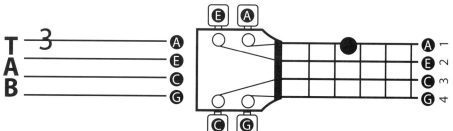

In TAB a zero on any line means you play the open (unfretted) string.

🔊 **Track 01**

As is in classical music notation (above), we read TAB from left to right and use the vertical bars to organize the TAB notes into spaces called measures. When two or more numbers are stacked on top of each other those notes are played at the same time. Often chord names or diagrams are shown above TAB notes. *Remember: Play only the notes indicated in the TAB.*

There are some basic techniques that are used in the songs and exercises in this book.

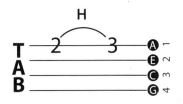

The Pull-off

Place your *2nd finger* (middle) on the *third fret* and your *first finger* on the *second fret* of the (1st) string. Strike string one and pull your *2nd finger* (middle) off the string to create the second note. Strike the string one time only!

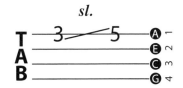

The Hammer-on

Place your *1st finger* (index) on the *second fret* of the (1st) string. Strike string one and "hammer" your *2nd finger* (middle) on the *third fret* to play the second note.

The Slide

Place your *3rd finger* (annular or ring finger) on the *third fret* of the (1st) string. Strike the string, press down on the fret and *slide your finger* from the *3rd* to the *5th* fret.

Exercise: Get down on some Blues

In this exercise play the *Pull-off*, *Hammer-on* and *Slide* techniques as indicated. Notice how similar the notation for each technique is when comparing *Standard Music Notation* with *Tablature*.

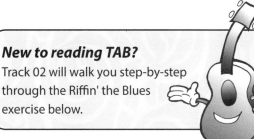

New to reading TAB?
Track 02 will walk you step-by-step through the Riffin' the Blues exercise below.

🔊 **Track 02**

Riffin' the Blues
Pull-offs, Hammer-ons & Slides

Learning the Secret Techniques

Learning how to use your thumb independently from your fingers is a key to playing fingerstyle. Try the exercise below. *Alternate between thumb (p), index (i) and middle (m).*

Track 03

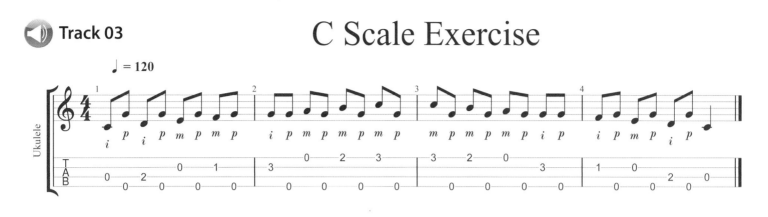

C Scale Exercise

There are three techniques that are used extensively when playing fingerstyle guitar; the Pinch, the 2-finger Claw and the 3-finger Scoop.

The Pinch

The *Pinch* is used to grab two strings at the same time. The pinch can be executed with the thumb *(p)* and index *(i)* or with the thumb (p) and *(m)* middle finger.

The Exercise below is designed to help develop your Pinch technique. Alternate between the thumb/middle finger, and the thumb/index finger.

Track 04

The Pinch

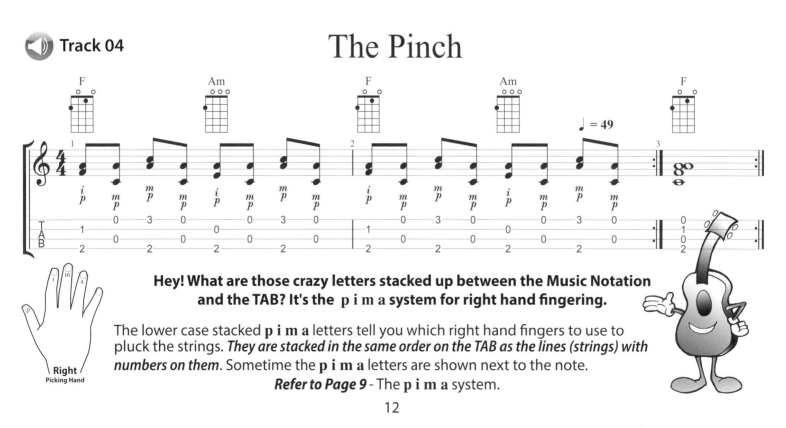

Hey! What are those crazy letters stacked up between the Music Notation and the TAB? It's the p i m a system for right hand fingering.

The lower case stacked **p i m a** letters tell you which right hand fingers to use to pluck the strings. *They are stacked in the same order on the TAB as the lines (strings) with numbers on them.* Sometime the **p i m a** letters are shown next to the note.

Refer to Page 9 - The p i m a system.

The Claw

The *Claw* is a technique that uses the right hand index and middle finger together to grab string sets that are next to each other. Your thumb generally is used to strike the (4th) string while the index and middle fingers together grab the (1st) & (2nd) string set or the (2nd) & (3rd) string set in a pinching motion resembling a crab's claw closing.

Play the example below using your thumb (*p*) and the two-finger (*i m*) Claw.

Track 05

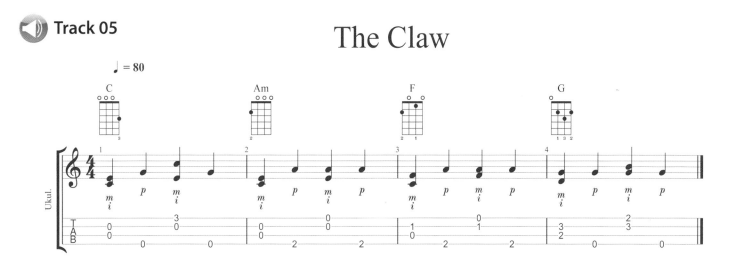

The Scoop

The *Scoop* uses the (*i*) index, (*m*) middle & (*a*) annular (ring finger) to grab the 1st, 2nd & 3rd string set. The thumb is generally used for the (4th) **G** string.

Play the example below using your thumb (*p*) and the three-finger (*i m a*) Scoop.

Track 06

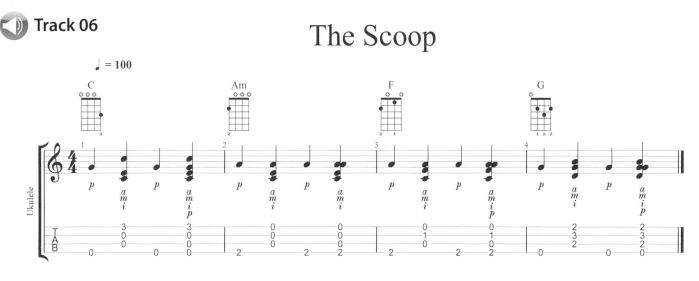

Picking Patterns
Ukulele Style

A picking pattern is a right hand technique where the strings are played in a sequence (or pattern) that repeats. These patterns can be used to make your chord progressions more interesting and fun.

Think of your right hand picking pattern as if it were an engine in a car. The motor keeps running as you drive from one chord to the next. *Don't let your engine stall!*

We will be using these 4 chords to practice our picking patterns.

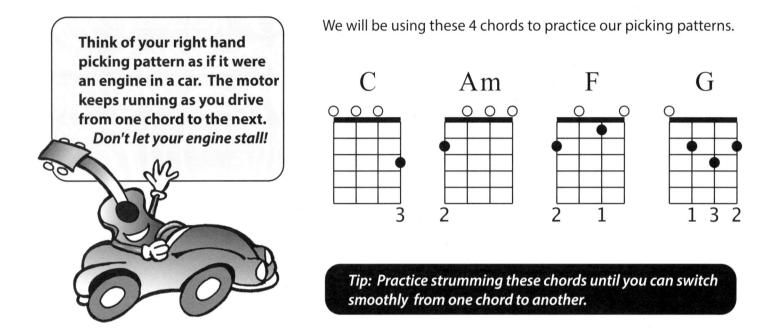

Tip: Practice strumming these chords until you can switch smoothly from one chord to another.

The following Picking Pattern exercises were designed using the *same 4-chord progression* with different picking patterns. All of the notes you need are in the chord above the measure.

Remember the *p* is the thumb, the *i* is the index the *m* is the middle and the *a* is the ring finger.

Cheaters never win and Winners never cheat.
Use the correct right hand fingering!

🔊 **Track 07**

Pattern 1
The "Go To" Pattern

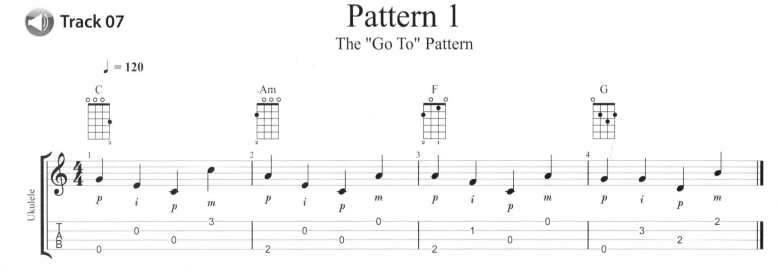

🔊 **Track 08**

Pattern 2
There And Back Again (String order 432 123)

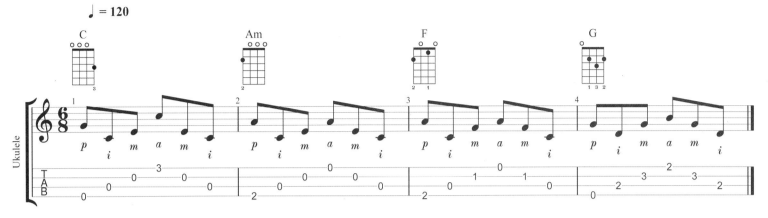

🔊 **Track 09**

Pattern 3
Pinch & Roll

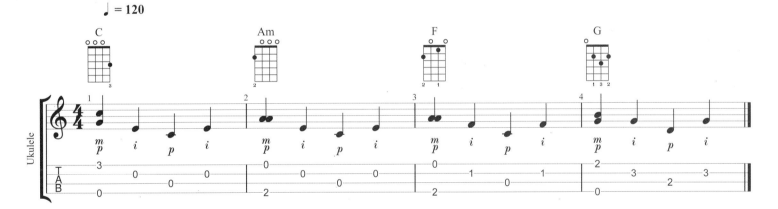

🔊 **Track 10**

Pattern 4
Outside - Inside

Picking Patterns Using Different Chords

These exersongs™ use new chords played with picking patterns using the Pinch, Claw and Scoop techniques.
You can adapt picking patterns to your own songs.

 **Track 11**   ## Progression 01 - Hit The Road Jack

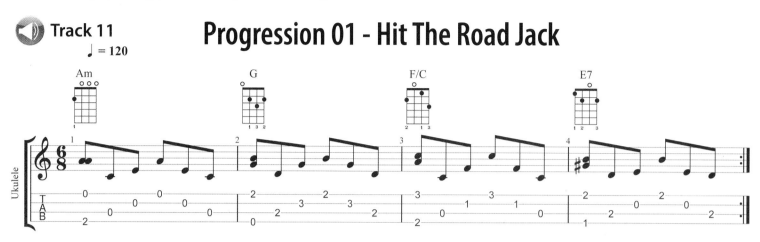

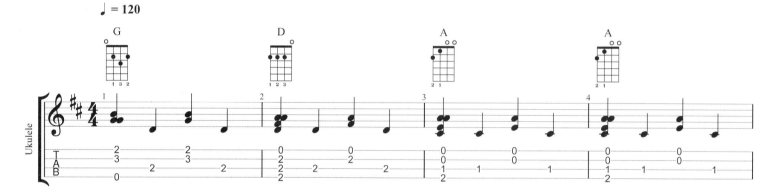 **Track 12**   ## Progression 02 - Pop Anthem

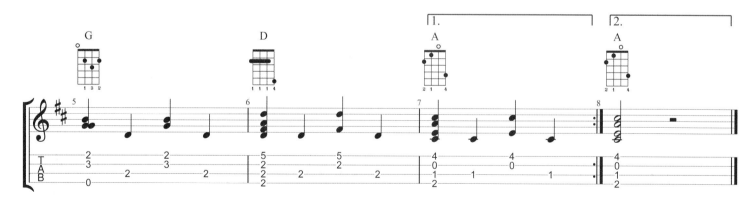

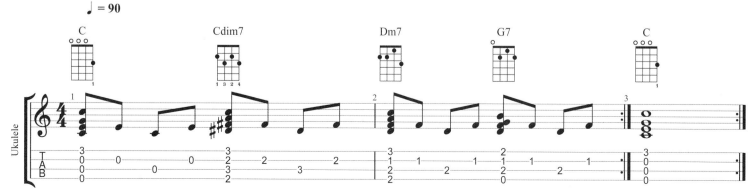 **Track 13**   ## Progression 03 - Jazz Turn

 **Track 14**

Progression 04 - Wagon Wheel

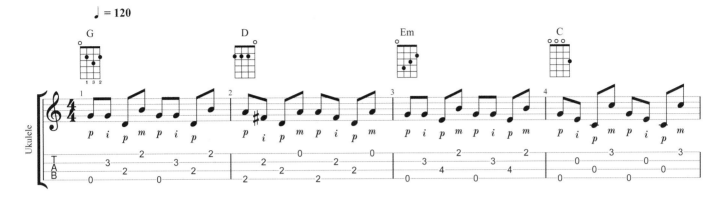

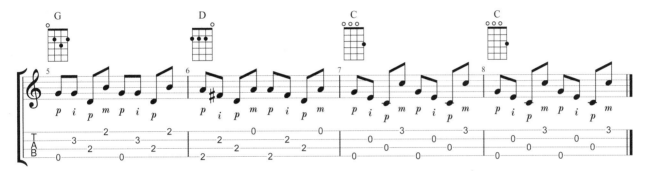

 **Track 15**

Progression 05 - Hallelujah

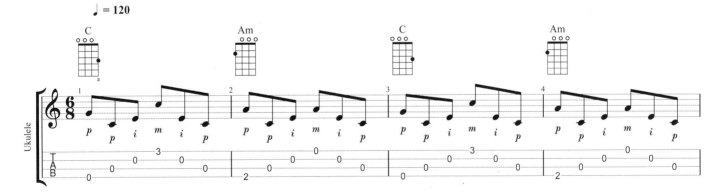

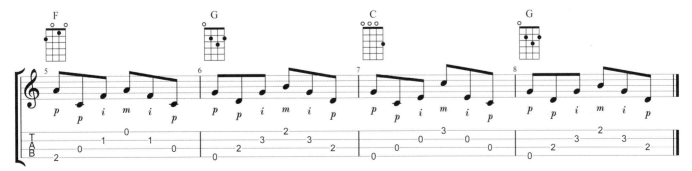

 **Track 16**

Progression 06 - Can't Help Falling in Love

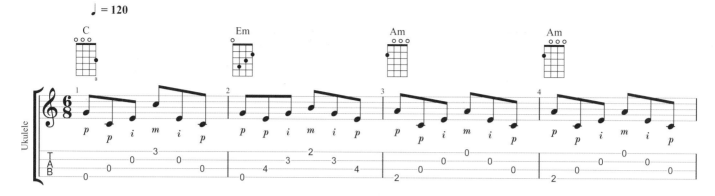

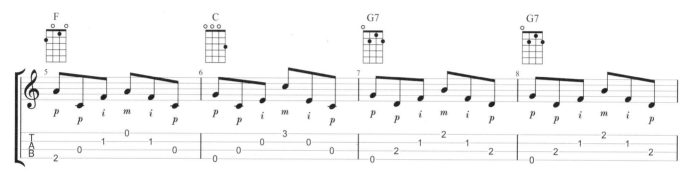

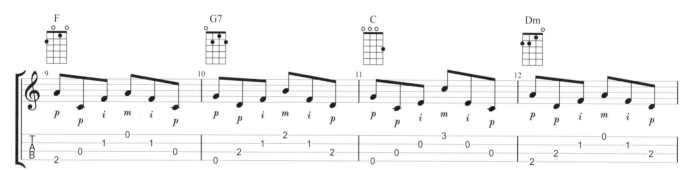

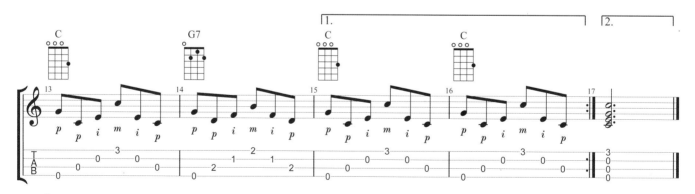

- **Picking patterns can be used for many songs.**

- **Many songs use more than one picking pattern.**

- **Picking patterns are often combined together to make more complex compound patterns.**

18

Building your Skills with Exersongs™

It's time to try out your new skills. The following exersongs™ were created to help you build your fingerpicking skills.

Play each example using the Claw, the Pinch and the Scoop techniques.

Practice Makes Permanent. Use correct position and good technique.

🔊 **Track 17**

Dynamic Duo - Using the Claw and the Thumb

🔊 **Track 18**

Little Bird

19

Nice and easy. Mosey-on-through this exercise, partner. Your third (ring finger) presses down on the third fret of the **E** string and stays there until the cows come home or the tune ends.

Track 19 Yippee Kai-Aye

This one looks harder than it is! Make an **F** chord and drop your pinkie onto the **C** note (third fret of the **A** string). Simply move the chord up two frets and pick the same pattern....the rest is easy! Imagine that.

Track 20 Imagine That

Use the *outside pinch* an the *i* (index) and *p* (thumb) roll to put the romance into this piece.

Track 21 A Melody Unchained

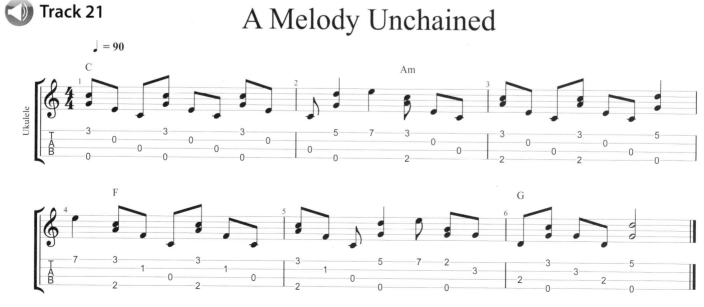

This is a fun classic ukulele Intro and Outro in the Key of C.

Track 22

Aloha Intro & Outro In C

Get your groove on. Make sure you stay in time when you do the slide techniques (page 11).

Track 23

Uke a Boogie

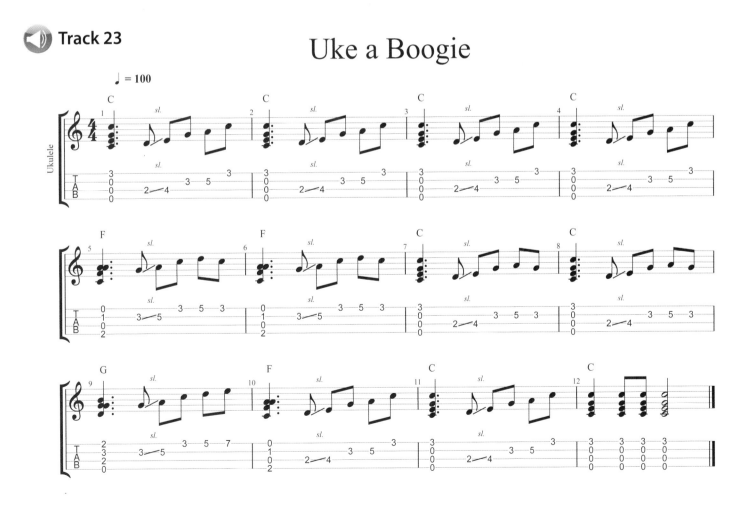

This tune showcases a classic melody with the use of chords and single notes. Practice the chords shapes first and then play the arrangement with both chords and melody.

🔊 **Track 24**

Shenandoah

Traditional: Arranged by KEV-Kevin Rones

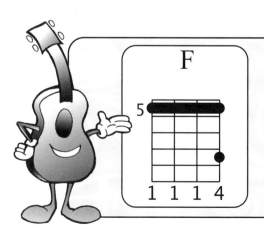

F

5
1 1 1 4

A Barre is created by pressing one finger across several strings on the same fret.

The **F Barre** chord shown in this example is formed by barring the index (1st) finger across the 5th fret and using the pinkie (4th) finger to reach the note on the eighth fret. The number **5** to the left of the chord diagram represents the fret number in which you place your index finger barre.

This exersong™ has a picking pattern that uses alternating string sets.

Track 25

Aloha Dreams

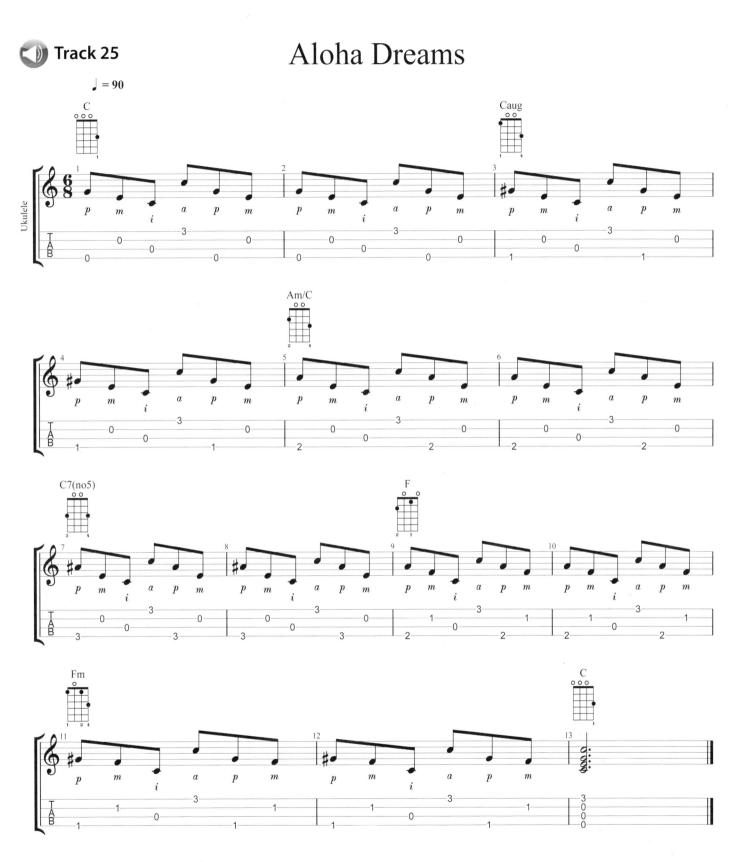

Gypsy Dance

Traditional Celtic tunes are often in 6/8 time. In 6/8 time each measure has the equivalent note value of 6 eighth notes.

The following three songs have a short measure of "pick-up notes" at the beginning of the song.
*Start counting on the first beat of the second measure.

*Counting 6/8 time
After the pick-up notes
count **1** 2 3 **4** 5 6
The emphasis is on
the *first* and *fourth* beat

Track 27

Celtic Ditty

🔊 **Track 28**

The Irish Washer Woman

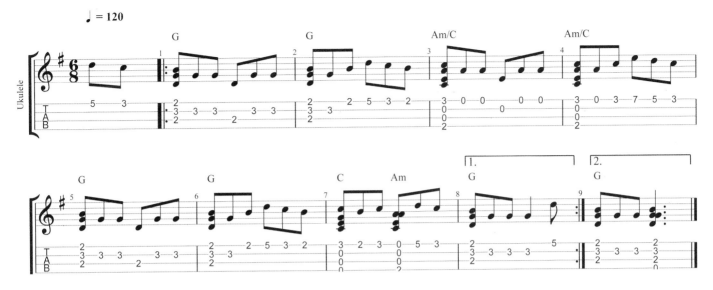

Swallow Tail Jig

🔊 **Track 29**

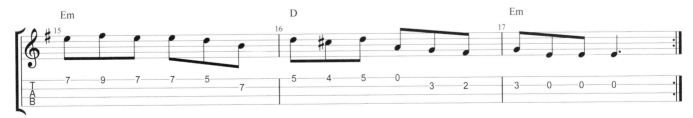

 **Track 30**

Ukulele Blues in C

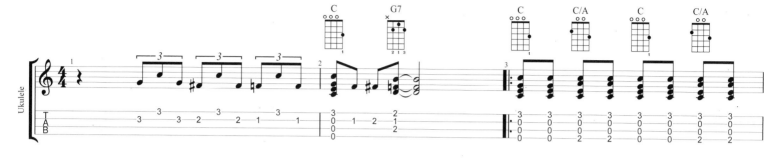

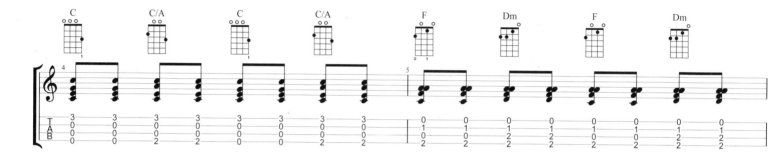

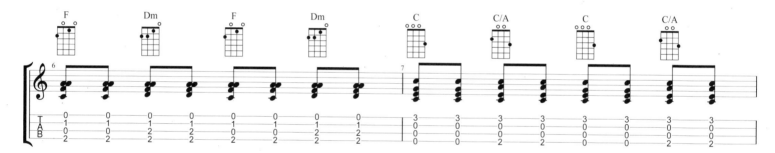

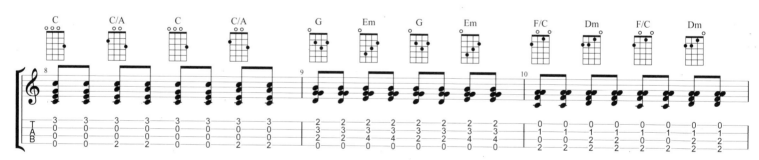

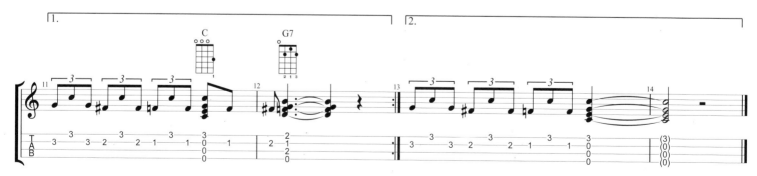

Track 31

The Hall of the Mountain King

Edvard Grieg (1843-1907) From the "Peer Gynt" Suite

Arranged by KEV

 **Track 32**

Danny Boy

Music by Rory Dhall O'Cahan (c.1600), Lyric by Fred Weatherly (1913)
Arranged by KEV-Kevin Rones

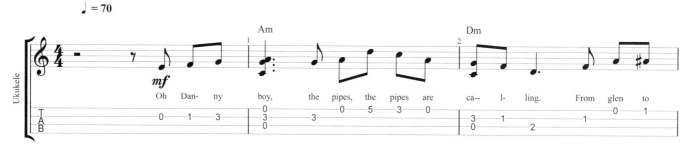

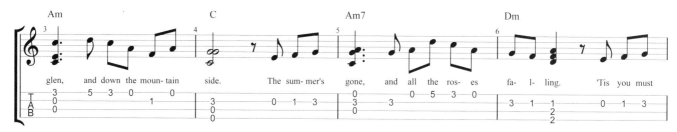

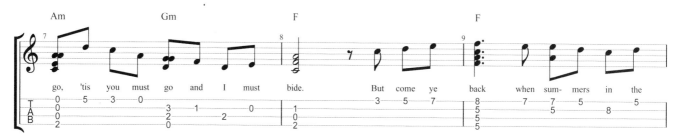

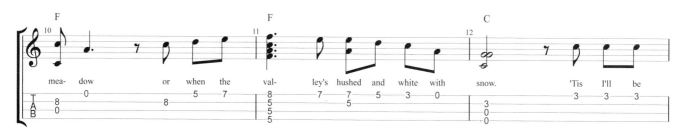

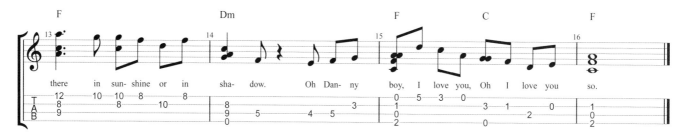

Minuet

Johann Sebastian Bach (1685-1750)
Arranged by KEV-Kevin Rones

Notes on the Fretboard

Each of the numbers represents a fret on the ukulele.
Use this guide as a reference to identify notes on the fretboard.

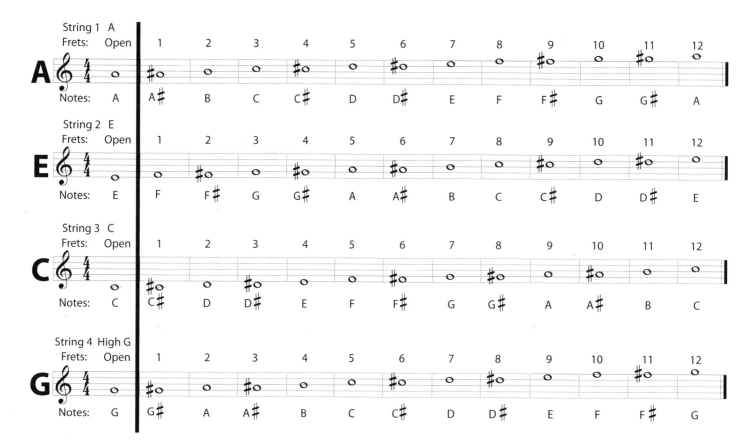

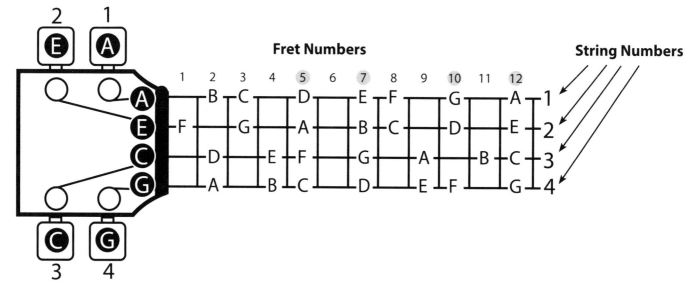

Use these notes for C tuning with a low G string

Where Do You Go From Here?

1   Watch some **BONUS VIDEOS** for this book.
https://thetikination.com/FSU1book

2   Get the next book in the Fingerstyle Ukulele Series
Fingerstyle Ukulele 2.

3   Get Quick Links to purchase these books online at https://thetikination.com

Check out these other
QuickStart Ukulele Books
available online and at
fine music retailers.

*Don't see it in your local
music store? Ask them to
order it from Hal Leonard!*

---

4 # Join the Tiki Nation Ukulele Community

Learn Ukulele the RIGHT way, have fun doing it. Make Friends, have even more fun.

Join our *Small Yet Mighty Ukulele Community* where players go to *Live, Love, Learn & Play Ukulele*

Join **KEV's live Online Ukulele Classes** at **TheTikiNation.com**
Get the details and Class Schedules at *https://thetikination.com*

Check out the **Tiki Nation Awesome Ukulele YouTube Channel**
Link to it at *https://thetikination.com*

Listen to the **Tiki Nation Ukulele Podcast** on iTunes
and Spotify. Get tips on how to become a better ukulele
player. Link to it at *https://thetikination.com*.

**Become a member of the Tiki Nation
and get access to:**

- *Our growing library with hundreds of ukulele lessons*
- *Access to Tiki Social Groups*
- *Exclusive Member Live Webinars*
- *Live events and more!*

https://thetikination.com